MW00774830

SPECTRAL EVIDENCE

POETRY BY TRISTA EDWARDS

ART BY GUY

APRIL GLOAMING

-First Edition

Publisher's Cataloguing-in-Publication Data

Edwards, Trista
Spectral evidence / written by Trista Edwards / art by Guy
ISBN: 978-0-9882061-9-9

1. Poetry: General 2. Poetry: American - General I. Title II. Author

Library of Congress Control Number:

For Aaron

Contents

Contents

Why do you come, yellow bird?

Abigail, *The Crucible*

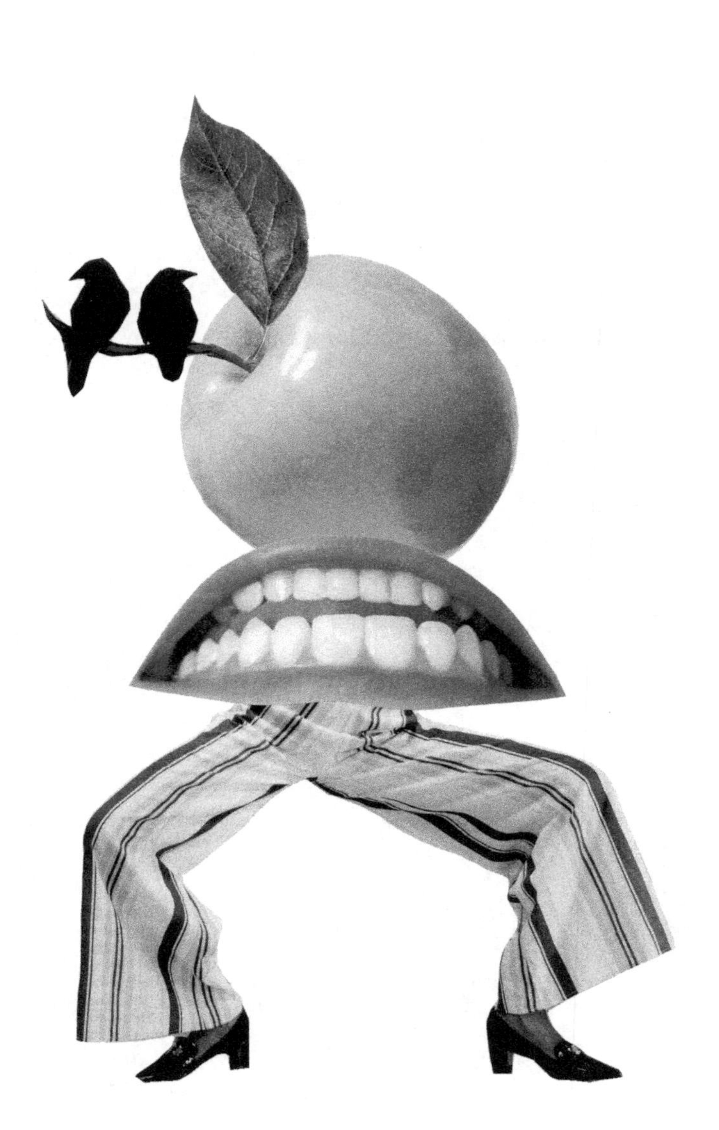

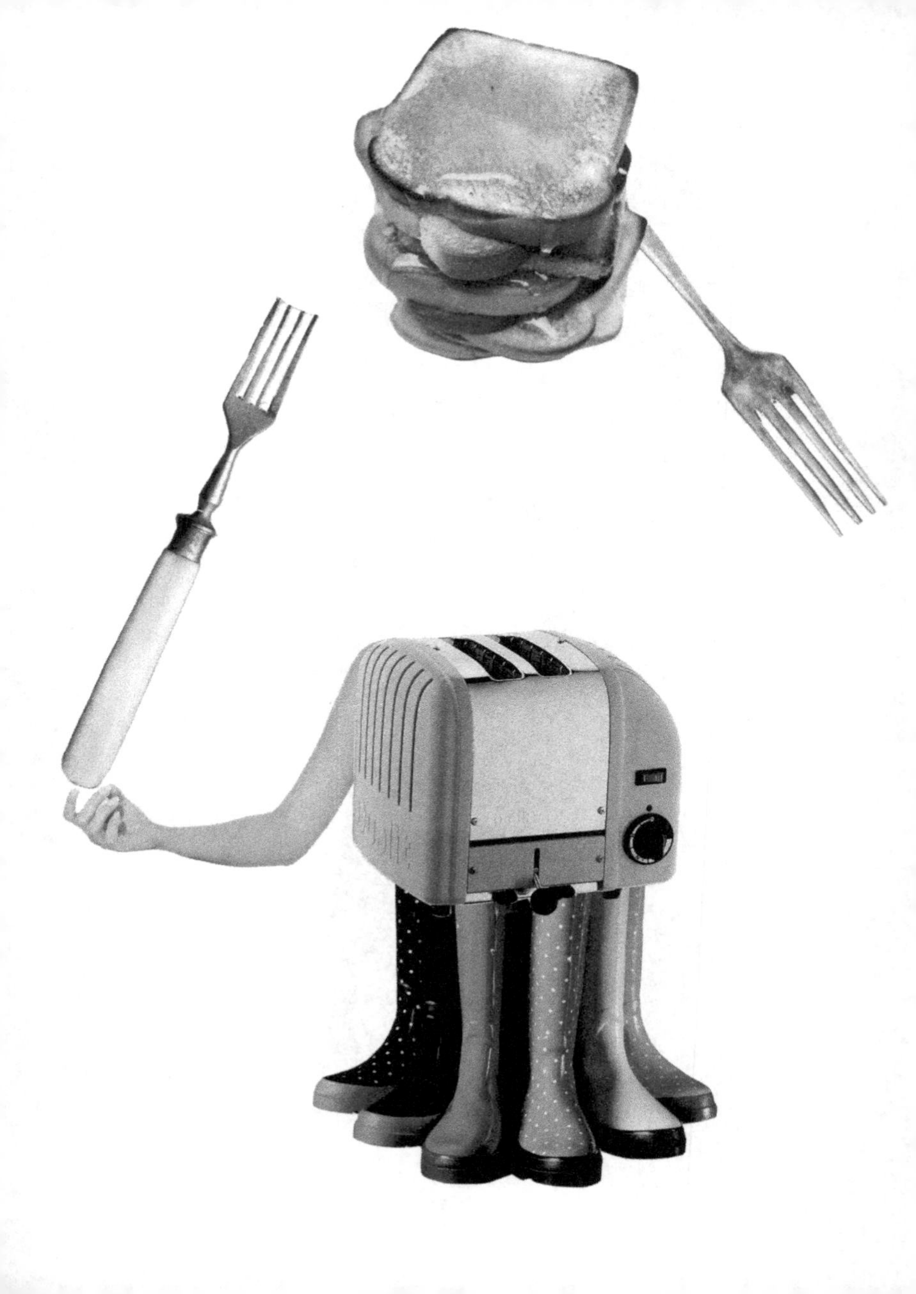

Equinox

The journey of history begins with hunger,
the reach for an end. The orchard's

in a vertigo of leaves. Halos fall
about their mothers. When every apple,

every dappled blood-red orb, offers
a little world, a lysis, you take it.

Thoreau once said, the gun gives
you the body, not the bird.

& so this orchard gives you winter,
not the apple. The molded, hewed world

of bodies in parallel formation.
Don't we want the body?

Just yesterday another boy took a girl
behind a dumpster & used her.

Her body reaching for flight
as the boy mauled her like carrion.

Thoreau was wrong. There is no body
without the bird. When we pull the trigger

& snap the ripest apple from the branch, come at it
with teeth, are we not asking for punishment?

The Moment We Wake

It begins as an insoluble chill
inside the body, then hair whitens.
Feet trample over a grave.
I hope this sounds mysterious to you,
not everyone is interested
in the foundation of dreams.

In a hotel last night
a child the size of a maple tree
painted a spotted horse
on a brick lighthouse & told me
it was the portal to all my splendor.
This night is not nocturnal.

Everything remains well-lit
under the slivers of my eyes.
Even now, as the child glides
a wet brush over dimpled stone,
I wonder how she'll escape.

Little Bird

It comes out of nowhere
like a fever, this shadow
that flits in my brain
whispering bad deeds
so base and petty
I can't help but wonder
how good it would feel
to hurt you. Here it is:
I lay still in bed,
project myself back,
years ago, to a party.
In a dark bedroom,
I find your body
passed out, slumped
in a chair. The little bird
lands on a pair of silver
shears so bright they shine
like a moon in my hand.
You rustle but do not wake.
The tangle of hair nesting
around your head is what
I came for. Those long tresses
calling to be hacked
& chopped so we could
both be ugly & powerless.

The little bird pecks & pecks
at my eyes until all that guides me
is the crisp sound of the blades
slicing into your mane.
The best part is nobody
will find us & I can finish the job
& leave you to find yourself
torn, as if by ghost.

Spectral Evidence

Yesterday, a fifteen-year-old girl was called a slut
because she held a boy's hand at school. She said
she hears it every day not because she has sex
but because it is the only word remaining

when people are at a loss for words. How many
girls believe this? That they hear a word
& they are that thing, that there is no real
difference between their bodies & a vision

of their bodies? That when a young man cries
to a court that it was her shape that overtook him,
that the vision of her skirt or breasts
was enough to send him into convulsions

there's allowance for his actions, his body
he could not control. What does a girl do that pinches
& bites & chokes at throats until we gasp
& point to brand her with our anger?

What is it that we see coming in the night
that afflicts us & proves her body
is ours to curse until the disease takes hold?
She says there is a ringing in her ear

that won't go away. She doesn't understand
why there is no cure. She knows the word
is all you become. Its innocence dismissible
against the evidence of shadow.

Salem

To deny is confession, an admission to rebel.
To save not the self but the sense of self

rooted in the heft of a name.

The body betrays, becomes a poppet
to language, takes part in invisible crimes.

We are left to make sense of shadows—

toil to discover what no one has ever seen
& forge a fire hot on the illusion.

The guilt of our bodies hunts us down

until bewitched we accept the scaffold.
We who are sentenced by a word

but swing for private treasons.

What is more condemning than the story
we conjure in the name of redemption?

What good survives the noose?

Even in death, a self persists,
a weight in the letters of a dead man's name.

The shadow of *witch* casts a spell.

Breaking Eggshells

To believe an eggshell can sink a ship
is to give into the confluence of events

or to believe that we are all characters
in some god's cosmic reverie. Could it be

science to say, eggshells should be broken
to prevent those with ill-will?

What wronged sailor etched the captain's
name into a dome of white? Deep in the hull

of the ship the sinking begins. The frying pan
left, careless of destiny. This must be the way

war begins. From the scraps of a tiny feast,
indignant peasants pilfer the pig trough

for royal remains. A silver arc of nail
lodged in orange rind becomes a ceremony

of defeat. Wound of kingdom. Anointed
with magic, a king falls by his own hand.

Below the Tower

There is a begging inside you—
it starts in your feet. They throb

with destinations of sleep.
Sleep congregates & hangs

in your begging hours, gone
underground, next to the bell.

Nothing rings underground
except the broken bodies

of St. Dymphna's sleepwalkers.
The church greets the ground

with its last brown brick. It wants
to say: *Beg for this. Beg from deep inside.*

Grand Collaboration

In the horror of the last hour, we recognize
the need to destroy the tower. To let the monster

pull the lever & choose to endure
the blank page. *We belong dead*, he says.

But were we ever really alive or just imagined?
Bodies of voiceless words set to life

only when summoned. His mate voiceless.
We are never complete. We are patchwork.

A floating city stuck in half-sleep,
disguised as assembly. Somebody gazes up,

says, *Look at that beautiful creature*.
Nothing's there. Our vision is too small

so we hand off our eyes, our way of seeing,
to more intelligent animals & tear the pages

from every book. The only thing that's complete
is the saga of everything we have yet to learn.

Boy Beaten with an Elder Stick

The most painful state of being is remembering the future,
particularly the one you'll never have.
Søren Kierkegaard

We are stunted by our own ghosting.
The damage is not what happens
but the residue of happening.

Once, an old woman leaned in,
smelling of anise & wet dog,
to say—cut a piece of elder on which the sun

has never shone & between two knots
hang it about the neck as cure
for St. Anthony's fire. For *falling sickness*—

cut a twig into nine parts & each night
burrow one in the hollow of your cheek
while you sleep. But what of the boy?

The boy who never grows? His height prevented
in the untold story of his growing—
unstorying, forever-reaching, beating.

Coven

We feel them before we see them,
those bats that dive & swoop
around the pole of light.

We are ten. All whoop & holler.
The farm at night cradles us in noise—
bark, whinny, the lunacy of crickets.

It haunts us & so we hurl rocks
straight up in a fit of giggles & howl
when a bat soars in, mistakes a rock for food.

The instinct of echo makes it swerve
just in time. But then we derail one.
We thought this is what we were

willing to do—to trick. Brand fire,
disrupt orbits, little heretics
crashing in the dark. Our smallness

crumples at our feet. We inch toward
the soft mound, bat brought to earth,
& form a circle around what we summoned.

Augury

Night-flying white moths are the souls of the dead, who in this form take farewell of this earth.

The girl was one of two
but not as you would think.

There were twelve sisters, Ivy,
the youngest named after the oldest.

Spiraling charcoal tresses
sticking against the sweat damp

cleft of neck. Who all night
cast out the blood of a vile gut.

Sickness spread in the valley,
swag-bellied sows heaved

in fits & died. Rain withdrew.
The farm died. People died.

Ivy died & laid white
then purple, for a week.

Those left buried her.
The oldest sister, her origin,

blued in sorrow & with nothing left
to fly, planted the last arrow

in the dirt. But then the moths
came. A collection so white—

a colony of hovering ghost-light
above her grave. At twilight,

the town mines the coffin.
They hope the winged serve

as a sign. They break the door
of where she sleeps. Breathless

tangle of hair, onion-white bone,
& dust. The sister points

to the sky as a deliverance of clouds
begins to drip a cure of water.

All the moths vanish. The darkness recedes
just as if some god opened the door.

Other Markings

For twenty bucks Mother Dora takes us one-at-a-time
behind a tattered brown curtain, peers into our upturned

palms resting in hers like stacked clams. At the kitchen
table, I fidget in a rickety chair as her finger tips

planchette my intersections of heart, wealth, fate.
On the counter, an upturned jam jar gleams

in the dim light, the muffle of a television wanders
from down the hallway. Her husband, who greeted

us at the door has vanished. Something simple happens—
I look up into her heavy, freckled eyes so winter-filled

like two tortured mountains & ask *who has read your*
future? Her fingers stiffen & pause. The television

echoes louder as if its only job is to jab & pinch the air
harder when it feels neglected. She says the *sun has intersected*

your union line. This means something moves in the marrow
of your bones that makes you guilty of ruin. I wait for her

to say more, to acknowledge my question
but she rises, crumples the twenty-dollar bill,

crams it into a rusted coffee can. *We are done now,*
she says. But I am not done. I want her to collapse me

with stories caged in my flesh, to pluck out my prayers,
those rare chants that mask themselves as the sound

of fear. I want truth to well in my cupped hands
& trickle down my arms like blood seeking re-entry.

But what I want most is to know what I will abandon
to save myself. What subtle voice, be it television

or crow, will call out to remind me of the all-too-quiet
world? Which bone is the softest & how will it break?

Shrikes at Black Mass

On the drive to the church, I undo my blouse.
The madness of the Georgia heat too much

for modesty. *What will you sacrifice?* I ask
from the passenger seat, sweating summer's

sweat under a humid moon. The church is back
in the pines, forgotten & rotting—molting, even.

Layers of damp leaves, rusted car parts, a corroded
Maytag freezer left sleeping on its side.

Inside the hollow of the freezer's exposed belly,
critters breed in nests made of wet earth.

Among the broken pews, hacked & splintered,
wallow mildewed hymnals. *We'll have to bring our own*

Christ you say noticing the outline of an old cross,
saved or stolen long ago. An old woman once told me

shrikes are the souls of those who assisted the crucifixion.
Those who hear the shrill of these winged

wandering souls are sure to meet misfortune.
I wonder what's trapped inside us?

Who will stumble after our cries,
meet us in some dark forgotten woods?

Our voices strident & butchering
the hazy sky like a million beating wings.

Ant's Egg as Antidote

Consider, more precisely, the composition
of an ant's egg. All alabaster, all pearl.

Inside, three castes—male, female & worker—
but which will harvest all the love?

Each egg pure opioid. Overdose.
Kill-switch. There is a beautiful sac I have so

simply declared yours. I practice hating it
to survive. Even the queen will eat

her own wings as a source of protein.
Her body so available it is not a body.

I have been here. I have ingested more.
& more. Bone & heart,

the viscos of summer, hair, honey
& clay, the toxin of memory.

How quick endorphins fade & from this
tiny egg we fall out of love,

out of each other's bodies. Here,
look at this hill of sand, as tall as a child—

inside is a kingdom of remedy, a lysis,
an antidote, a cure. Wing-eaters we become,

high on the pupae of past love. Let us
forget, let us survive, let us dine.

Child Weaning & the Migration of Birds

Infants, they say, weaned in late autumn,
experience the seasonal waning of daylight,

depart from their mothers' breasts into a period
of acute loss. By autumn, all the magpies flee.

They surge across the sky. Blur of little wings.
Because the lake glistens & ripples below,

the flock looks down & sees itself.
They fly toward it, all dumb-luck & thirsty

for the shiny reflection. It is almost child-like
how they recognize their own faces,

caught off-guard then inexplicably greedy
for more of themselves. If only all of us,

when we were once young & suckling,
our first tooth budding through, bit & broke

our mother's skin to taste the warmth of where
we came from. If only we could recognize

this moment as our daylight fading, our own
bitter reflection disguised as migration

in which we journey nowhere but into a shiny lake,
diving into ourselves until we drown.

Palmistry

So it gives us everything, this death,
this grace, our crime against the tomb.

The mother died, half her body turned
dark, verging on a form of murder.

We must learn to die, the father said,
execute a sly rebellion in broad daylight

& write our names in the dirt. Beneath
the nightstand are the letters we keep

precisely to keep us sad. We can't stop
reading. That is what we do—return.

We visit the dark body, the bed
where the mother caught fire & wait.

In this hour of grace, we wait to wait again.
Each word a little death. *We will write this one day,*

the father said. We will feel the glow.
We will read our own dark hands & wither.

Burning Pornography in the Woods

Have you ever built an entire city
out of sunlight? Have you asked

what the burning meant
or cupped a toad like an apple doll,

charred & wrinkled? We burned
our women in the woods,

or rather their likeness.
I laughed at the sight of their fiery

consumption. We were only ten,
playing with dolls. We purged them,

purged what we could become,
conquering a body, the idea of a body,

not yet ours. Alone we braved,
two little girls with scorched hands.

Harvest Child

Yes, even children cling to the piths
of nostalgia, that root rot that begins

before it can be seen. Like that first sharp
tinge in your tooth before a cavity.

Truth is, we get used to the soil
we eat, the grime that coats the lungs,

the throat, the teeth. It spreads
with the bite of each apple

or some such sweet confection
that drops from tended grove.

When I look at the sky I can't stop
imagining the angels, how they drift

above our heads like birds
robbed of their instinct to fly.

When I bite into a speckled orb,
I taste the acidity of every apple

that ever passed between my lips—
always hungry for that original sting.

I can't stop divining the orchards.
Eating something sweet means

bitter disappointment, eating cherries
means *illness*, spilling wine in the garden

means *trouble ahead*. Once, I swallowed
a whole pit, not by accident

as I told my mother, but because
I wanted to swap one canker for another,

to plant my own hardened shadow.
There is no cure for what takes hold.

When I think back to that first bite,
breaking the skin was most delicious.

Carl Zeiss

Dedication

I have walked miles of suburban ghost towns
in the early October of the Georgia foothills,

past the posters of vacant, garish smiles
promising a kind future. In any house

or horror flick, a family portrait waits
for the flesh of its contents to return.

In any horror flick, or house, flesh always
finds itself elsewhere. I want to beat down

doors, break windows, overturn the dead
plants, brittle & stubborn in their pots.

I want to enter into some still, abandoned life
& confuse myself into believing

it's mine. This is a choice I make.
At the bottom of a hill I find a phoenix,

or rather a dedication to the bird, vibrating
its oranges & yellows from a tattoo magazine.

Its crest of feathers inked in such red guilt
it would be my betrayal to look away.

An Extraordinary Delivery of Rabbits

Mary Toft (1701-1763), an English woman from Surrey, tricked doctors into believing she had given birth to rabbits.

First it looked like a pig's bladder, then a cat's paw
& afterward rabbits, one after another.

Eleven in all fell from her warren. Creatrix of colony.
Mother of mothers. An inedible feast unto herself.

Taken before she could coddle the wet fur, before she
could lick her lips in anticipation, the doctor pickled

their slack bodies & lined the jars on his mantle.
Stillborn meat poisons the blood. So many believed

this to be true. A country woman births a brood of rabbits
So many said she was hungry. Starved.

& when she lost her unborn child in the field,
a cunning woman offered her a story, so as she would

never want again—You will give birth to rabbits.
You will take the claws & body of a cat, the head

of a hare & insert them into your open book.
Make this story yours. Ink it in the blood of your womb.

Sin Eating

Trichophagia, or Rapunzel Syndrome: the compulsive eating of one's hair.

On the second floor of the Mütter Museum,
in a sea of matted red carpet, encased in glass,

a placard tells the tale of a father who bargained
away his unborn daughter, haggled with a sorceress

so that his wife could eat the planted rows
of the witch's garden. The daughter's hair

long & doomed as Porphyria's, a strangling
prophecy around her little throat. Imagine

if she ate her hair, as another placard suggests,
before any prince came. Imagine consuming

your father's desertion, your mother's curse.
Your body a poison of pica, a descending

rope of toxin snaking down the throat.
Think how she could have harvested

herself, ingesting fate like a peach pit,
a hard, corrugated past. Would she

have been better off dying of her own sin?
Would her mother have still chosen hunger?

Overripe

Lately, everything ends in flowers,
yet we need so little of their petals,
voiceless silks. Just coolness we take,
lay our brows to like a frosted pane.

Children enhance our distaste
of invented landscapes, too overripe,
even the birds neglect the lines
of juice sliding down the rind.
Catching the glare of dying flora,
I return to the proper names
of roses, their sad fate I adore more
than their assorted conceptions.
I have found sufficient the fracture
of our bodies, that place of questioning.

Museum of the Rarest Colors

I. Mummy Brown.

The man who daubed you into the iris
of Nimue's gaze learned your origins.

Not just pitch & myrrh but bodies—
bone, flesh, jarred organ of Egypt. Civilization

squeezed from a tube. *Caput mortuum*,
to alchemists. *Worthless remains, dead head.*

He buried you beneath the hollyhock
avowing never to paint your raw umber

in a snarl of a beggar maiden's hair again.
You are a museum. More than a gob

of bitumen tombed in some dalliance
hanging from a hook. You're revival.

Until you are buried again or wrecked in a fire.
Each time your color blends & bleeds with dirt.

II. Brazilwood

You stain the notes of Bach—
Partita in D minor for violin no. 2.
Your high shine glazing the bow's
brasilin—

pigment crafts an ink of sound,
rubicund in appearance,

forsaking in strain. You, the woebegone
first wife of genius. The Royal Court
Composer. I wonder how much red
stained the bend of my grandfather's
Appalachian fiddle—

the one my grandmother sold
at a tag sale. I saw it once
but memory's faded as sheet paper.
Maroon—

your particular shade on the panels
of his pick-up, the one always loaded
with deer carcasses, wide-eyed & fixed.
The maroon pick-up—

that slid off the ramps as he tinkered below
& all your color left his body. Your music
running out of his hands.

III. Cochineal

You are the crushed waxy hull
of a parasitic beast. Found leech
to the pad of prickly pear cacti,
scraped remorseless with dried, black,
lopped-off tails of mule deer.

You're an orchard of crimson pearls
set to harvest, dry, & flatter
the carmine frosted lips of a maiden
kiss. A smeared maquillage of eggs,
the weight of a thousand tiny deaths
rouged into the pucker of lounge bar
sirens. You are meant to protect,
a ruddy shield to keep creatures at bay

but only when still husked in the body
of your maker. Caked on the mouth,
you are the color of weapon. Sorcery.
Beguiling. Mark of the witch.
In Medieval times women who crimsoned
their lips met the same glow in flames,
consumed in a ball of rosy heat.

& like the heat, you keep coming back.
Painted targets on the strident maws of warriors,
Diviners casting spells & chants. *Heed me,*
they say, *heed all that this color brings.*
You, you the wrath of ancestors, ghosts.
I stain my lips with warning.

Offering

Saint Louis Cemetery No. 1, New Orleans, at the tomb of Marie Laveau.

Once a hairdresser you are now a pilgrimage—
Voodoo queen among bleached vaults, mausoleums
stacked with anonymous bones. We travel

to you a clatter of tourists, our sweat a badge of dedication.
If not rain, then palmetto bugs take these bodies,
declare them not fixed but migrant—

lacing through the cracks by water or legs.
Marie, I only have these almonds
but they are yours. I have no secrets

but I give you this kiss. I kiss you among the Xs,
little scars that litter your tomb
like some wayward map. My lips

against the heat of your stone. Your shrine
draped in beads, peeling from sun.
But no, I do have something to tell you—

Marie, once the summer wouldn't let go. Its heat
didn't recede into autumn. It balled
into a tight fist & stayed at my side.

Once, a man laid all his weight on mine
until our shadows closed like curtains.
He pressed his thumbs along the valley

of my throat. I could taste the air leaving my body.
Metallic & bitter as if some delicious wine.
When I was almost empty he let me go,

my body calling out prayer for a flood,
to carry me into a world of endless streets. I tell you
this because your breath is gone.

Because although your tomb is littered with cakes,
bourbon, lipstick, I wonder if you long to taste
what is not so readily given? To press your lips

to thorns of wild blackberries, the gentle snag
that rips open a heat of blood? I know the burn.
The emptiness of a mouth searching for salvation.

Persephone

In a kingdom of poets, she walks through Hell.
Her body a fracture, a book split open.
The horror is not the underworld but the act
of splitting—her body a cracked bridge.
A story between two worlds. She is conduit,
never architect. Never creator, only created.

In the story where she kills the lion,
a dead white dove falls repeatedly from the sky.
She cannot repair it. Only the story grows stronger.

Hair of the Dog

For My Brother

I told the boy his brother was buried out past the barn,
under the old chicken coop. The coop itself was long gone

but its cracked foundation still marked the earth.
I told the boy his brother lived & died before the boy

was born. The small child with all the heart of a newborn cub
believed this. The boy asked what his brother was like.

I told him his brother did all the things the boy did not
want to do. That he was good in every way good can be.

That he was bright in every way bright can be. That he died
suddenly & nobody knew why or how but they knew

he was under the coop. The boy asked how I knew
& I said because this is what I feel & when we feel

enough it is true. The boy asked if we could bring his brother back.
I told him we would need hair of the dog, to lay on the crack

in the foundation where his brother slept. The boy whimpered,
afraid that the crack wouldn't spit his brother out

but close & his brother would stay under the coop forever.
I asked him why he thought this would happen. Because, he said,

I feel it. I picked the boy up, cradled his soft head, damp with sweat
but hot. His hair smelled of sugar maple & campfire.

I held him for a long time until he was nothing but a little fox,
squirming in my arms. Then he bit. Tiny ruby specks

emerged above my wrist. I dropped him quick & angry.
Off he scampered into the crack, down into his brother's world.

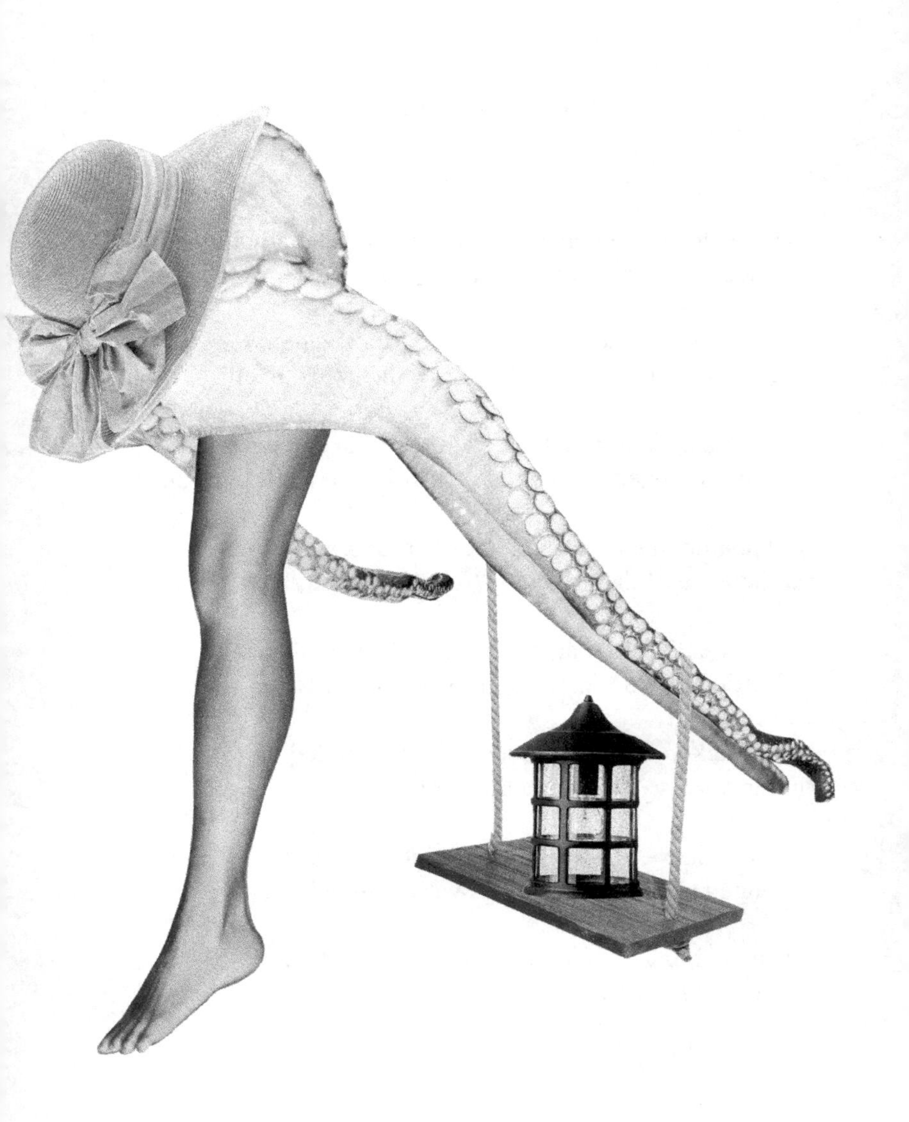

Holding a Dying Creature

At the close of the dead-end street gleamed a boulder—
our lectern, our pulpit, our highest hill.

Because she lived alone in a house by the boulder,
we deemed her a witch. Or was it the house itself,

dark & stagnant with the caged raccoon in the garage
that we shrieked our young girl shriek at as the sun fell

& the animal's bright, fixed eyes found us daring
at the edge of the driveway? That summer

we quit eating in search of magic. The devilry
of jutting hipbones. A conjuring valley of ribs.

Heat flickered off the pavement, tar bubbled
in the cracks. We invented his murder—

the imaginary boy who crossed into her yard,
wronged her in his trespass. We conceived

his hand hung from twine from her backdoor.
We dared each other to steal it. & do what?

This useless hand, vulgar in its lack of need
to touch us, held our bodies glimmering

with sweat & our newfound spell.
We took turns mounting the rock

to wave our hands wild in the gloom
of evening, pretending it was our incantations

that brought on the first drops of rain.
We wanted to frighten & be frightened,

to invade & take that invisible talisman.
A conquest of our power, to shed

the creature of our adolescence.

Bellow

After Ada Limón

Tell the hunter & all his hounds,
the rabbits they chase down the hill,

the blacksmith's sooty iron hammer,
the sparkles that fly from his strike;

tell them all the myths are true.
I am rabbit. I am those tracks

they follow farther into the wood
under growl & starlight & branch.

Tell my mother I'm bound in iron,
chained to the stake & set to burn.

Tell all the women they can
inhale the smoke of my skin, hair,

heart—that it will root inside, deep
in the belly like a heavy daughter.

Tell them I will squeal under the heat,
that the scorch won't be silent, that Satan

blackened my soul so there would be
no blister. & they will tell their children.

I was but a name. A scapegoat. A girl.
For this I burn. For this I bellow.

Sounder of Pigs

It's some November night on St. Mary's river.
The moon screams its bright white,

a feral hog's shriek assaults my ears.
This morning, we crossed into town

to buy earthworms. Now we stand,
baiting our hooks in the dark.

I twirl the worm around thin curved metal
without looking, a muscle memory I never knew

I had, & jab the plumb, noiseless body
over the tip. The man at the bait shop

chawed musky tobacco, a deliciousness
of saliva & disregard I will never taste.

You know, dem hogs crash thru the pines
faster than spilt 'shine, tear you up just'n

bad too. If'n you find ya self in a thicket
of herd'n boar, don't holler or nuthin,

just let 'em ride thru. Dem tusks will'n carve
you up nice if you take to wail'n.

It is not the hogs I'm afraid of,
it's the punishing way you lay me down

on the sand & tell me that I'm not allowed
to enjoy it. Not the crisp air that raises my flesh.

Not the weight of your body as it enters mine.
Even now, in winter, the mosquitoes hum

from stagnant water & make a host
of my body. Their need more tender

than yours. To pierce & take only
what they need, as little as they need.

Bridegroom's Lace

I have seen catastrophe disguise itself
as ceremony. One foot after another,

down the aisle until they meet their mark.
A bride sneaks a peek at her lover's shoes—

he has left one lace untied. The black aglet
ticking out some Morse code as he rambles

into a future where she cooks daily breakfast.
But tonight they join in virginal bonding.

Their untold story beginning
to story, to tie itself into a double-knotted

vow. When they can't untie it, they'll cut it.
They will each take a piece of the broken lace,

tie it to a different one, aching
with the phantom of that old knot.

Letters From Mayhayley

Mayhayley Lancaster (1875-1955), a Georgia lawyer, political activist, midwife, teacher, fortuneteller, and assumed witch, writes letters to: Celestine, a journalist; Ferrol, a friend and medical doctor; and her mother.

I. Dear Celestine—

Two months now & it don't let up.
Yesterday folks was lined up to the hen house,

least that's what I could make out the good eye.
Got a new marble piece in the other.

Folks quit staring but last week a child hollered
when he seen it & his mama left

before I could give her numbers to play.
I know, Celestine. They want answers.

They want husbands. & the menfolk want
high yields come fall or lost cows or wives

to come waddling home. I tell 'em payment's
all the same—dollar for me, dime for my dog.

Boy, do they pay. I got so much paper
I'm stuffing it in the coop. The sun ain't stopped

shining on me or this godforsaken shack.
The creek's dry & the clay's cracked.

They want rain, Celestine. But I tell 'em
it's a born gift, not a learned gift.

I weren't born to make it rain. I can only make
when it's coming. Sometimes I think how I've seen

more children in the lines of their mamas' hands
than Noah seen water. How people want plenty

until they got it. Not but a few hours ago,
some gal—itty bitty thing, hardly bleeding—

came in wanting the number of her babies.
How do I take that dollar, Celestine, & tell her five

but ain't but one gonna make it? How do I
say & for that last one you'll swap heartbeats?

Celestine, how can I make myself un-see
all the children they pay me to heed?

Cordially,
M

II. Dear Ferrol—

When you think about it, we both heal folks.
Probably both hurt folks too. You, a soldier

back in France. Me, here in Georgia. Hell, we're a pair.
Regular misfits, I suppose. But you're a man.

Your version of healing ain't what scares.
It ain't witchin'. See, Ferrol, what I forgot

to mention the other day when you stopped in
was that I've been healing folks since I's a girl.

Longer than you. But that don't matter none.
People see my marble eye & long coat

& they make up words for what I am.
My medicine's different, Ferrol.

It's numbers & stars, babies & lost rings.
Cards are my instruments, my stethoscope

into souls. Some wanna hear what I see
so they come with dollars & dimes

to feel better. To win. To find love.
Ferrol, forget what you know about the heart.

All that pumping. All those chambers.
Folks stay alive on the blood of hope.

This is science, Ferrol. It's why you came
to see me. To see how an old granny

out in her shack can cure so many
with so little. But heed me,

it's not nothing. It's just something
man finally wasn't born to know.

-M.L.

III. Dearest Mama—

You've been dead twenty years now
but I just wanted to let you know I'm okay.

Lots changed, Mama. Me & the world.
Remember that raggedy boy down the street

said I done sold my soul to the devil?
That I stood over graves, put one hand

atop my head & the other to my boot
& proclaimed—*Everything between*

these two hands I give to you, Satan!
That never happened, Mama.

But you know that. You know I was born
different. That I's meant to heal folks.

I tried, Mama. I got into the law
& tried to save that Jewish boy from hanging.

He didn't kill that girl, I saw it in his hands.
They only wanted him to swing for being

different. I got into politicking. First woman to run
in the state legislature. I wanted schools

& railroads & free doctors for new babies.
But they didn't want me, Mama. When I tried

man's way—books & courts & trials—
they just told me what I was. Woman. Witch.

I went back to my shack but I didn't stop.
& when that man came looking for his sow

I pulled a card & named the crook who took it.
He killed that thief, Mama.

& they came for me. I had hexed him
some said. I had made him do it.

I didn't do it, Mama. But you know that.
My words rang true. I sat in the box

& pointed to the killer. Said—that man,
that man right there. He came to me

with a dollar & a dime so I pulled a card
& off he went to find the man

who took his sow. Papers ran stories—
Witch's Words Not Used in Court Since Salem.

Imagine that, Mama. I, a learned woman
of the law. Nothing but a heretic. Indebted

to Satan for knowing what they know & more.
But this is what I've learned most, Mama—

Hands don't lie, just the men they work for.
& when men don't like what their hands hold,

they wait till everybody else looks away
& shove 'em deep in their pockets.

From across the way,
Mayhayley

At Dusk

I can smell the molten newspapers.
A brown tabby jumps the chain-link post,

carries off a chicken bone.
I can hear the chatter of raccoons

as they pilfer the trash.
Then a squall—some owl, maybe a bobcat.

I stand at the window
& search for the glint of eyes.

I can't find the dog.
This moment has no name.

Down South

The chapel is empty even when we are in it.
There are no angels here, only kudzu.

It does not surrender. We do not burn.
We are too out of reach to feel the heat.

I followed the vines up the steps & broke
the rectangle of glass to let myself in. It is easy

to follow history for what has yet to happen.
For desertion. A thousand blackboards

can't illustrate the answer. History books failed.
One day, we will realize we held the cure

all along. Our hands will put out the fire
& we will clog the wounds with mud.

It will be said, we will be done.
The kudzu will take over. Let it.

Descent

We all have names but they are not
who we are. We shed labels, strap on

titles, fall sick to slurs. This little utterance
we proclaim tumbles from our mouth

& binds us to story. We didn't choose
these letters, these arrangements,

but we go to war for their weight
in honor, the great gold of heritage.

What tongue will curse our bodies
with the jinx of elocution?

Will we burn among the ruins
for the blessing of others?

Not all can hide their banner
& sometimes it isn't the screams

that point the loudest, but the silence
that descends after the wail.

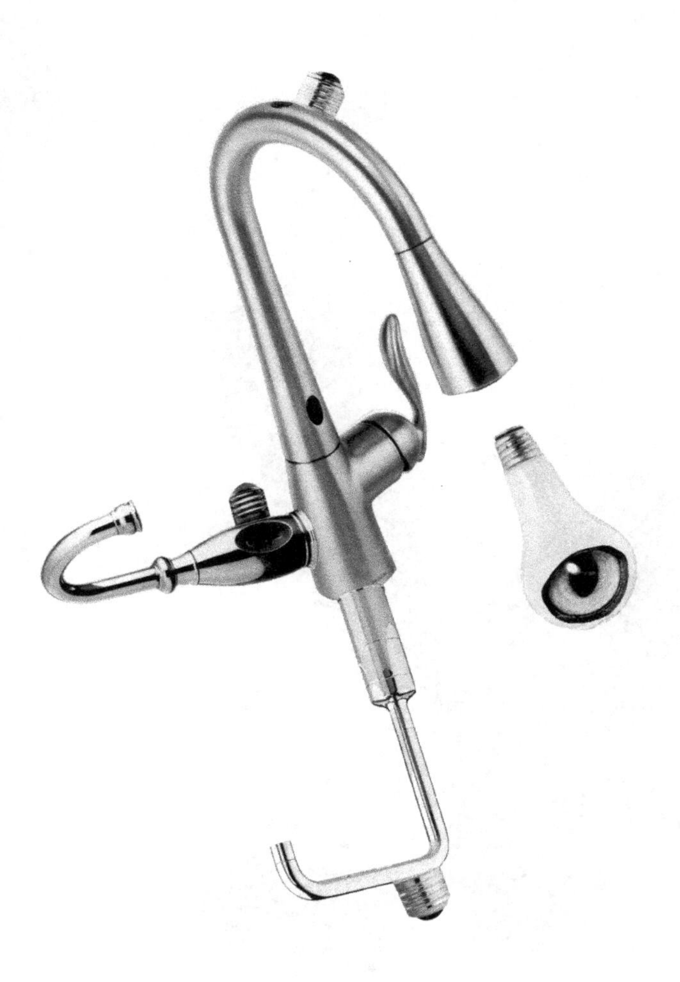

Editors

Poetry Edited by:

Emma Peterson Cardiel,
Robyn Leigh Lear,
& Lance Umenhofer

Art Edited by:

Robyn Leigh Lear

Notes

"Bellow" borrows its title and structure from Ada Limón.

"Grand Collaboration" pulls the line "*We belong dead*" from the 1935 James Whale film, *Bride of Frankenstein*.

"Ant's Egg as an Antidote," "Boy Beaten with an Elder Stick," "Breaking Eggshells," "Bridegroom's Lace," "Child Weaning and the Migration of Birds," "Hair of the Dog," "Holding a Dying Creature," "Sin Eating," and "Augury" all borrow modified text and titles from *Tell the Bees...Belief, Knowledge & Hypersymbolic Cognation* distributed from The Museum of Jurassic Technology.

Acknowledgments

My gratitude goes to the editors of the following journals, in which the poems in this book, sometimes in earlier versions, first appeared: *The Adroit Journal, Bad Pony, The Boiler, Eclectic, Quail Bell Magazine, Luna Luna Magazine, Midwestern Gothic, Moonchild Magazine, Occulum, The Southeast Review, Sou'wester, Stirring: A Literary Collection, Venefica Magazine*, & *Yes, Poetry*.

About the Author

Trista Edwards is an Ohio born, Georgia raised, and Texas livin' poet. Trista is an associate editor at *Luna Luna Magazine*. She is also the curator and editor of the anthology, *Till The Tide: An Anthology of Mermaid Poetry* (Sundress Publications, 2015). You can read her poems at 32 Poems, *Quail Bell Magazine, Moonchild Magazine, The Adroit Journal, The Boiler, Queen Mob's Tea House, Bad Pony, Occulum,* and more. She creates magickal candles at her company, Marvel + Moon (www.marvelandmoon.com). You can also read more about Trista at www.tristaedwards.com. She lives in Denton, Texas with her husband and her two pups. This is her first book.

CPSIA information can be obtained
at www.ICGtesting.com
Printed in the USA
JSHW011325130920
7673JS00007BA/167

9 780988 206199